The Blessing Of Simple Gestures

Gestures

Nourishing the Relationships
That Brighten Our Days

The Blessing of Simple Gestures

Nourishing the Relationships That Brighten Our Days

Aleta Harris

ELM HILL

A Division of
HarperCollins Christian Publishing

www.elmhillbooks.com

The Blessing of Simple Gestures

Nourishing the Relationships That Brighten Our Days

Published in Nashville, Tennessee, by Elm Hill, an imprint of Thomas Nelson. Elm Hill and Thomas Nelson are registered trademarks of HarperCollins Christian Publishing, Inc.

Elm Hill titles may be purchased in bulk for educational, business, fund-raising, or sales promotional use. For information, please e-mail SpecialMarkets@ ThomasNelson.com.

Library of Congress Cataloging-in-Publication Data

Library of Congress Control Number: 2018966993

ISBN 978-1-400325030 (Paperback)
ISBN 978-1-400325047 (Hardbound)
ISBN 978-1-400325054 (eBook)

To my treasured friends.
You inspire me, encourage me, challenge me, comfort me,
make me laugh, and share my love of life.
I can't imagine what my world would be like without you.

I'm into encouragement. I'm always the one clapping loudest when someone is running hard for the prize. You can hear me yelling, "Great job!" or, "I'm so proud of you!" There is power in the gift of encouragement, and if you will indulge me, I would like to share with you some unique ways to deliver it.

I love it when someone expresses joy over a card or gift that I have given. A friend recently told me she has every card or note I have given especially to her. She says she periodically spreads them out on the table and finds renewed encouragement as she is reminded she is loved, valued, and that her life has purpose.

Every gift, card, or brief note is an opportunity to share what is in my heart as I celebrate birthdays, holidays, and "just because" times with friends and family.

We each have unlimited opportunities to lift spirits, celebrate the race of life, bring smiles to tired and discouraged souls, and remind people they are not invisible or forgotten, because people need to be reminded that they are remembered, loved, appreciated, and valued.

It is for that same purpose that you picked up this book. You want to make a difference in someone's life by making every gift, every card, meaningful and remembered as it encourages its recipient.

So let these ideas inspire you to creativity and bring your spirit of encouragement to life. The world needs you!

Aleta Harris

Contents

Celebrating Friendships

Especially at Christmas

This N' That

Post-It Notes

Celebrating Friendships

COVERINGS

We are careful to cover the things we cherish and want to preserve. I pray that this table cover will remind you that you are covered by:

God's great grace. He delights to pour out His undeserved blessings on us.
God's tender mercy. He is pleased, not to give us what we deserve, but He tenderly gives to us extravagantly.
God's peace and joy. It is indeed a peace that passes all human understanding and a deep joy that no one can take from us.
God's promise. His promise never changes and it keeps us focused in a world of many distractions.
God's profound love. Who can understand it? It is too big, too deep, and too wide to comprehend, but we cling to it in this life and will continue to do so in the life to come.

So, my friend, <u>you are well covered</u> by a God who cherishes you and protects you. Be blessed on this, your special day. **Happy Birthday!**

Suggestion: Attach this to a gift of a tablecloth or any decorative covering. It can be adapted for birthdays, Christmases, or just-because gifts.

Friendship Is a Sweet-Smelling Savor

As the years pass, I cherish even more my friends and the friendship we share, for I believe that friendship is one of the greatest blessings that God gives to us. And so, just because, I wanted to give you a small something that would remind you that you are cherished, that you are "that sweet-smelling savor" who brings joy to my heart, and that I thank God for you. I ask Him to bring blessing into your life as you seek Him and His perfect will for your life in the days to come.

It's not much, and it surely won't last forever, but I trust that our friendship will, and that God will be pleased as together we love Him, serve Him, and anxiously await His return.

Holding your friendship close,

Suggestion: Attach a tag with this greeting to a gift of perfume or bath gel. This is easily converted to a birthday or holiday gift by changing the graphic and closing.

Friends Make Us Sharper

How blessed we are,
How sweet the living
As we give thanks
For friends God's given.

Friends make me sharper. They do. Really, they do. And they do it in various ways.

Some friends sharpen my wit with their warm and crazy humor. They make me laugh from my heart and I somehow forget about the issues of life that often weigh me down.

Some friends sharpen my life with their penchant for style. Fashion, for them, is an expression of the classy lady who is sporting the matching purse and shoes (and earrings) and, all the while, demonstrating an air of elegant confidence.

Other friends sharpen my mind with their knowledge and their love for learning. They challenge me to be aware of what's happening in my world and contemplate the dangers of noninvolvement and apathy.

Others sharpen my life with their incredible creativity. Those are the gals who can craft a stunning gift out of discarded ribbons and bows, or wrap a gift so beautifully that I resist opening the gift for fear of undoing the exquisite wrapping.

Some sharpen my life with their "craziness"…their ability to be uninhibited and spontaneous, or to try a new hairstyle or a new exotic food. They are those friends who love to snap "selfies" with others in the shot and always wearing a huge smile.

There are those who sharpen my life with their wisdom. They lovingly share counsel from their cache of life experiences and from a genuine caring heart. They are guides on the days I am feeling doubtful or confused or lonely.

Some sharpen my life with their incredibly deep faith. They are the living testimonies of hearts surrendered to an awesome God. They bubble with joy and peace and show me that, even in the depth of difficulties, those qualities prevail and carry each of us through to sunshine again.

You sharpen me. You make my life fuller and richer, and I thank you from the depth of my heart for a friendship like that.

Suggestion: Attach a simple pencil sharpener to the top of the card to adapt it to the gift purpose.

Magic Eraser

This →

is an authentic magic eraser.

With it you can effectively erase the negative effects of all that, in the past, has robbed you of moments and days of sunshine and peace in your heart:

- The word spoken in haste
- The thoughtless deed
- That financial issue that threatened
- The unexpected medical diagnosis
- The silence of a friend

Hold it tightly in your hand and watch it as it runs smoothly across the cache of memories tightly guarded in your heart, erasing the sadness and the hurt of those difficult times.

Well, we know that this eraser is not really magical. But we are reminded that God, in His great love for us, sent His Son Jesus so we can have hope beyond the often inescapable heaviness of life.

We find that quiet place, close our eyes, and hear the voice that silently reminds us of the Omnipotent, Omnipresent, Omniscient, loving God who desires to live in our hearts and who is able and anxious to erase the sadness, the confusion, the doubt, the fear, the sin, and all that would seek to fade the joy and cloud the promise He has given to each of us.

So may this eraser, friend, remind you that there is a Savior, Jesus Christ, who we can trust to do all He has promised. We daily celebrate His life and know that He came to show us how to live and to love.

Have a blessed day! I pray that in each day to come you will experience His presence, His power, His peace, and His purpose as you look to Him.

You are loved and cherished,

Suggestion: Attach at the top a simple eraser reflective of the season or purpose (for example, Christmas, Easter, birthday, or just because).

Friendship Samples

Samples: Ya gotta love 'em!

We savor the tasty food samples offered us as we shop with the hopes that we will be impressed and buy the product before we leave the store.

The beauty product samples intrigue us and we massage lotions onto our hands, apply makeup samples or colognes to the back of our hands or wrists, or put the face cream samples in our purse to test when we get home.

There are cleaning product samples, seed samples, paper product samples... Well, you can add to the list.

How amazing it is that God Himself encourages us to "sample"! He says in Psalm 34:8: "Taste and see that the Lord is good; blessed is the one who takes refuge in him."

That is because He knows that once we experience His love, His grace, His mercy, and the hope and joy we find in Him, we are hooked! We want the entire fulfilling package, and He gives it to us freely and extravagantly.

This life in Him is delicious and satisfying.

And it began with just a "taste."

I hope you'll enjoy these samples. Know that I love you, friend, and cherish your friendship.

Suggestion: Gather cosmetic, gardening, and other samples to attach to this card.

Scented Hand Soaps

How could one properly introduce a scented hand soap as a gift?

We're looking for hooks…like:

- Clean *hands*, pure heart (Nope, too preachy!)
- Gotta *hand* it to ya' (Nah, too redneck!)
- From *hand* to mouth (Yuck, not with soap!) or
- *Hand* it over and no one will get hurt (Not even!)

Not workin'!

Let's try it from the perspective of how hands are used…like:

- Calming our children (or spanking them)
- Drinking a cup of rich hot coffee, tea, or milk (or Theraflu)
- Bowling, croquette, bocchi ball, shuffleboard, tennis, or arm wrestling (or golf for those who like to hit, walk, hit, walk, hit)
- For signals like "Hello," "Goodbye," or "I give up!" (I'm about to)

Nah! Not the intro I was looking for.

But this soap smells good,

it's practical,

it's personal,

and I bought it especially for you
because it's Friendship Day

and you are an exceptionally good friend, hands down!

Happy Friends Day! I love and appreciate you so much!

Suggestion: Attach the card to a bottle of scented hand soap and adapt
the greeting for Christmas, birthday, or just because.

PENS

Some people like to collect ink pens—all colors, sizes, unique designs, old and new, expensive and inexpensive, pens that once belonged to well-known people. They amass them, display them, and tell in detail the fascinating story of each uniquely different pen. However, it's very interesting that, though they enjoy owning them, they do not use them. And a pen not employed in its intended use is not worth much at all.

Our God-given gifts are like that. Unless they are used, they bring no glory to the One who gave them to us. They lie dormant, useless, like a watch without a battery.

I pray that you will use this pen, that you will write heartfelt praises and encouragements with it, that you will use it to put to paper your visions and your goals, your record of who you are in Christ.

Your gifts and your testimony have been recognized by friends and family. And so they have placed their confidence in you and look to you often for wisdom. I am grateful that you are using your gifts for His honor and glory and for the building of His Kingdom here.

You are deeply loved and appreciated,

Suggestion: Attach a pen (perhaps with a fancy notepad) with this card.

Seeds for the Harvest

We have planted, watered, and reaped a beautiful harvest of friendship, haven't we? Our friendships have deepened and our circle of friends has been enlarged.

Perhaps you don't know what kind of harvest these seeds will give you, but I promise you the fruit they produce will be incredibly good. (Trust me.)

I challenge you to prepare the soil, plant the seed, water it, care for it as you watch it grow. Then share the harvest blessing with others.

Sometimes the seeds that God gives us to plant are unknown to us. But you can be sure that whatever He gives you will be good.

When you plant the seeds of faith, hope, kindness, trust, purity, encouragement, compassion, friendship, and any other good seed into the lives of others, you will reap good things in your life.

Think about it. Let me know what your seeds are producing.

Suggestion: A small terracotta pot filled with some potting soil, along with a packet of seeds, creates a special gift that makes your friendship "grow."

Doormats

I know… you are thinking, "What an unusual housewarming gift!" A doormat is certainly an unusual gift, but it does have great significance.

However, the kind of doormats people put on their doorsteps says so much about who they are and what they like. Sometimes it has a picture of a paw print or a nature scene or perhaps the emblem of their favorite sports team. Sometimes it has a monogram or a family name proudly displayed. But a doormat opens the door to see who the people who live in the home are and what is important to them.

I pray that, above all else, Jesus will always take preeminence in the home that you are making, and that you will proudly let those who come into your sphere of influence see that you serve Him above all. May the determined words of Joshua 24:15 proudly express your heart's desire to always seek to serve God.

Each time you enter into the house that you are making your home, may you remind yourselves, each other, and God that "as for me and my house, we will serve the Lord." And may it be your testimony to every person who will pass the threshold of your home so that they might see Jesus and His perfect will as the center of all that happens there.

You are deeply loved. And because I love you, I pray God's peace, His purpose, His passion, and His power on you and your new home.

Enjoy the years, the blessings, and the place in His family He has given to you.

In Him,

When Friends Move

Sometimes we don't like the things that life throws our way.

That's what I felt when you announced you were moving. And you're not simply moving to a nearby town or neighboring state, but you're moving far away, leaving countless miles between us. My heart was crushed and I spent considerable time talking to God about it.

Though my heart is saddened, knowing that I may not see you, I realize that far outweighing the sadness of you moving is the joy I have as we have shared a treasured friendship. We have cherished memories we hold close as we have laughed, cried, and worshipped together. My cache of memories is full and I hold each one close to my heart.

I will close my eyes, see your face, and I will smile. You have enriched my life. I recognize our friendship as a gift from God's hand. I have watched you navigate, with unswerving faith, deep disappointments and unexpected illness, daily trusting Jesus for strength and wisdom. You are an amazing teacher and I have learned from your example.

But friendship is forever, and you, my forever friend, will find yourself contentedly planted in another part of God's garden, where you will find blessing and be a blessing to others. We will continue to share, through avenues technology has provided for us, how God continues to lead us down pleasant paths that He is setting before us.

And so, I send along this scented candle. As you feel its warmth, enjoy it's light, and drink in the aroma, think of this friend who will forever bask in the warmth, light, and aroma of your friendship and influence on my life.

Holding on to friendship,

Suggestion: A scented candle is the perfect gift to include with this note.

Especially

at

Christmas

Friendships at Christmas

Friendships seem sweeter at Christmas. Maybe it's because we take a bit more time to say, "I appreciate you and what you bring into my life every day throughout the year." I enjoy the time I spend with my friends, sharing laughs and sometimes tears, discussing politics or fashions or music or food or a myriad of other topics.

I pray God will grant you, in this season and in the year to come:

- *a sincere faith* that you will hold on to with a death grip when tough times come,
- *a joy* that will bubble up in you and make you laugh out loud as you consider the blessings you have received from God's hand,
- *hope* that will shine like the noonday sun when the "stuff" of life tries to dim it, and
- *a peace* that is as unshakeable and profound as the love that God has for each of us.

Merry Christmas from me to you. Know that you are loved and treasured.

P.S. I found some interesting quotes on friendships and this is the perfect time to share them.

Walking with a friend in the dark is better than walking alone in the light.

—HELEN KELLER

There is nothing better than a friend, unless it is a friend with chocolate.

—LINDA GRAYSON

Some people come into our lives and quickly go. Some stay for a while, leave footprints on our hearts, and we are never, ever the same.

—FLAVIA WEEDN

CHRISTMAS LIGHT FOR YOU

In this Christmas season, we would wish you *light for your journey.*

> *Light* to *warm you* as you travel.
> *Light* to *warn you* as it reveals dangers along the path.
> *Light* to *lead you* when you doubt your way.
> *Light* to *leave you* with a sense of assurance and joy.

May this light remind you that *Jesus is the Light.*

> We pray you will *embrace Him*, the light,
> that you always *face this Light* so the shadows
> of life fall behind you.

Our prayer for you is that His presence,

> His peace,
> His power, and
> His purpose be yours
> as you boldly carry His light,
> that you cherish it and share it with others.
> Celebrating our friendship,

SMALL BELLS AT CHRISTMAS

It is the small bells that sound the sweetest, that create the truest resonance. Theirs are the peals that ring clearest, even amid the din that threatens to muffle or overpower them. They create the beautiful melody and accentuate the harmony of the songs as we carefully listen to their cadence.

Theirs is not the loud clamor, the sometimes abrasive clangs that distract and deter us. Rather, theirs are the tones that draw us deeper into the music itself, that magically carry us to the heart, the very core, of the One who calls us ever so quietly and sweetly to Himself through the music of the bells.

We pray that in this season and in the New Year that is quickly approaching, we will listen ever so carefully to the small, quiet ringing of the voice of God's Spirit as He draws us deeper into the heart of the Father. We pray that you will not be deterred by the distracting noises that would shift your interest to lesser things and make you miss the song He is playing for you.

He is most assuredly leading us to days filled with blessing and challenge and change and opportunity. He is calling us to help others who are frustrated and lost as they follow the deafening, confusing sounds of this world to hear the song we are hearing, to begin the journey that leads us to the Father's heart.

Let's journey together this year, led by God's Spirit song, and discover where He is leading us.

We believe it will be a most blessed year. Don't you?

CHRISTMAS SURRENDER

As we have contemplated the past year and asked God for a word of direction and challenge for the New Year, we keep hearing Him say, "Surrender." With that in mind, we looked again at the Christmas story and now understand more clearly why this is the direction in which He is leading.

We see Joseph and Mary *surrender* willingly to difficult requests from the mouths of angels, despite the obvious accusations and rejections of a community that did not believe or understand. And the shepherds as they *surrender* to the surprise visit of an angel that called them, saying, "Go and find." The magi *surrendered* first to the call of a star that they knew in their hearts would lead them to "the one who has been born king of the Jews." It was a long-term sacrificial investment of time, energy, and great material resources. They then *surrendered* to the voice in a dream that led them home by a different route, thus providing time for two faith-filled parents to escape the devious intent of a maniacal king.

Please take some time to ponder the experiences of others who surrendered themselves to God's direction and who, in so doing, made the first Christmas complete and consequently changed the course of history.

In this season and throughout the New Year, let us join those of the Christmas story by surrendering ourselves to His will, His way, His plan. It involves a bowing of the head and a bending of the knee, but it will change the course of history for you, for your family, and for those to whom God leads you.

Friend, may the One to whom you surrender dwell in you richly and live through you fully, bringing you joy, peace and, purpose.

We love and appreciate you,

Suggestion: A bookmark or small ornament with Mary and Joseph or the magi

A Christmas Song for
My Friends

"The Lord is my strength and my song; he has become my salvation"

(Psalm 118:14)

This Christmas we wish for you a song:

a song that will lift you when you are low,
and give you courage when you are tempted to fear;
a song that wakens you with joy in the morning
and infuses peace within you as you lay down at night;
a song that rings with more clarity the more you sing it,
and becomes the sole melody of your life.

In this season and always, we pray you will allow Jesus to be your song, your strength, your salvation.

Together singing the song of the Lamb,

"The Lord is my strength and my song; he has become my salvation"

(Psalm 118:14)

Suggestion: Christmas music or a printed copy of your favorite Christmas song

TREE BLESSING

May
your life
this Christmas
and throughout this
New Year be as a sweet
perfume as you live, and love,
and serve the Jesus who has blessed
us with His love, His grace, His mercy,
His forgiveness, hope, purpose, and courage
as we face
the future
with faith,
confidence,
and joy.

I just wanted you to know that I love and appreciate you and cherish the friendship God has given to us. Have a most blessed Christmas!

Suggestion: An ornament or a bookmark of a Christmas tree

The Church

It isn't just a building…a place where we meet to sing, or pray, or learn, or expound the Word. It isn't just where we come to share a meal or fellowship or even where we come to bring our praise or our petitions.

God's Word tells us that **WE** are the Church, the people God calls His own. The people called to be lights in a sin-darkened world, called to lead others out of the darkness of loneliness and despair into the light of hope and newness of life, just as we ourselves were once led out of that darkness.

We are reminded, at Christmas as we ponder the birth of a Savior, and in each day of the New Year, that we have been bought with a price… so that we can be the Church.

May this small ornament remind us to, together, **BE** the Church.

Praying His abundant riches for you,

Suggestion: An ornament of a church

"Come, Let Us Adore Him"

What a profound Christmas invitation to us… and it is an invitation for every day of the year!

"Come, let us…" It is not an individual call but rather a passionate call to corporate worship, to come together and to, as one, adore Him.

That is why we come—to worship together as family, as followers, as lovers of the One who came to give us life.

We are better together, aren't we? May this New Year find us together in worship of the One who longs to leads us into profound praise.

Serving together,

Suggestion: Find a bookmark like this one, or be creative and design one to insert with the Christmas greeting.

Small Graces
at Christmas

Such a tiny ornament, yet it serves to remind us that it is often the small things, the quiet and unobtrusive things in life, that make the difference in our days. A smile. A mere word of encouragement. A tiny candle in the darkness. A fire on a cold evening. The presence of a friend.

We pray that in this Christmas season and throughout this New Year, you will purpose to be a people of small graces, for they, in actuality, offer large doses of hope and healing to hurting and lonely people.

May this ornament encourage you to share the truth of a tiny baby, born in a small town, to a family of seeming insignificance, yet His birth made an immeasurable difference for us all.

Have a most blessed Christmas season,

Suggestion: Any small ornament or item of faith

THE JOURNEY

They journeyed to Bethlehem, obedient to the demands of the census. They journeyed to Egypt, obedient to the voice that led them to a new place and to safety. As they journeyed, their gaze was set forward, not backward, for they knew that God was calling them into His will.

In this Christmas season, we encourage you to journey obediently and resolutely into God's will, even when He doesn't reveal to you the destination at the onset of the journey. Don't look back, but fix your eyes on the adventure ahead. That's where you will clearly see Him and where He will empower you to be a part of something greater than you could possibly imagine.

The Christmas tune "Do You Hear What I Hear?" comes to mind. Why don't you hum the tune? Then ask yourself, "What do I hear?" Listen carefully. You will hear the voice of God calling you.

We pray that this simple ornament will remind you to run to Him and to know that He is calling you to great and wonderful things in the year to come. Let's journey together through this next good year of promise.

Wishing you God's abundant blessings in this Christmas Season and in the New Year.

We are blessed to be a part of this journey with friends like you,

Suggestion: Any graphic of Mary and Joseph on their journey, a copy of "Do You Hear What I Hear?" or other Christmas tune

Christmas Trust

If there is a singular word in this past year that God has brought into clearer focus for us, it is definitely the word "trust."

> We have trusted and He has been faithful.
> We have trusted and He has provided.
> We have trusted and He has journeyed with us.

Trusting God has always proven to be an exciting and often faith-stretching adventure.

TODAY we have decided to trust Him.

This approaching New Year will, we are very certain, draw us deeper into this trust where we will see Him more clearly, hear His voice more distinctly, and praise Him with our hearts full of gratitude and confidence.

We pray that you will, in this New Year of unfathomable promise, join us in recklessly trusting Jesus, the One who brings joy to the world, peace on earth, and good will to all men.

> "Surely this is our God; we trusted in him, and he saved us. This is the Lord, we trusted in him; let us rejoice and be glad in his salvation"
>
> (ISAIAH 25:9)

This
N'
That

I'm Watching You, Dad!

I'm watching you, Dad. I see what you do.
Sneaking kisses to mom and to all us kids too.
Playing ball, though you're tired, after supper is done
Fixing splinters and rockets and stuff that won't run.

Acting corny when our music plays in the car
Then making us laugh with your wild air guitar.
Being faithful to God and patient with others,
A good friend and neighbor, an example and brother.

So Dad, as I watch as in firmness you raise us,
Correct us, encourage and lavishly praise us,
Determined I am to be just like you
'Cause I'm watching you Dad, and I see what you do.

Suggestion: For Father's Day, pair this note with an inexpensive pair of sunglasses or binoculars.

CHILI

Thanks for the delicious chili! We enjoyed it tremendously, but I'm confused about the name:

> I really think that 'chili'
> Is a misnomer quite silly.
> The texture's rich, the flavor's bold
> But it is _anything_ but cold.

> "It ain't chili," I want to note,
> While I feel it burning down my throat.
> Oh, the peppers make it so much hotter
> As I reach again for my ice water.

> But I eat it all and lick the bowl
> And feel the burn down to my soul.
> Elated for the meal revered
> Yet saddened that's it's disappeared.

> So, thank you for the lovely dish
> Though 'chili', girl, it's not.
> I think I'll call it "happy burn"
> And return the empty pot.

Thank you for the WONDERFUL chili! Yum. Yum. Yum.
You're the best!

On Dining at Your House

We clapped our hands and shouted,
"Oh, what a dandy treat!"
When you called and asked us,
"Won't you come and eat?"

Now dining in your lovely home
Is something more than special,
For what you serve invited guests
Is *never* artificial.

The beefy stew so succulent
And veggies, not a few,
The homemade bread still soft and warm
And apple butter too.

And then you served the final course—
A choice of tasty pie,
Chocolate or pecan,
Whatever pleased our eye.

A dollop of some whipping cream,
"So rich!" we both commented.
Thus we returned to our home
Tummies full and quite contented.

But best of all, besides the meal,
That thrills us beyond measure
Is the common bond of love we share
That brings us lasting pleasure.

The richness of the food will fade
And finally come to end,
But our hearts and minds will always have
The remembrance of dear friends.

Thanks for a great meal and the best of fellowship!

On the Sad Loss of Your Tonsils

I write with deep condolence,
Profound, you must believe,
To learn that at the hospital
Your tonsils you did leave.

I know you've known each other
All your life long through.
And well, I guess that you could say
They were like a part of you.

How cruelly was done the deed
Such friends to separate.
With scalpel sharp and laser bright
Came their swift and final fate.

The doctors knew, I'm sure of this,
That your tonsils were quite ill.
No cure there was in time nor place,
In capsule or in pill.

And so I say this now to you,
I'd say it to your face,
Your tonsil friends had suffered long,
But they're in a better place.

So lift your chin and smile again
And enjoy the life you're given.
And know that your ever faithful pals
Are now in Tonsil Heaven.

On the Loss of Your Gall Bladder

The rumors out; it's ugly too,
The voices loudly hissing.
They're saying that while you've been gone
Your gall bladder is missing!

We feel so bad. What can we do?
We'll help at any cost.
We can't imagine what it's like
To have your bladder lost!

So know that we, your friends, do care
And we avail our time
To look as long as it will take
Your gall bladder to find.

(What does it look like anyway?)

Post-It
Notes

How God Sees Us

I love reminding my friends, when we get together for a meal or just to chat, that they are valued. Each lady receives their own copy of some funny pictures I have seen on Facebook or online, a humorous story, and a verse from God's Word that opens the door wide for me to remind them how much they are loved and appreciated.

One of my favorite memories occurred when I purchased, at my local Dollar Tree Store, a couple bags of alphabet beads, some attractive cords to string them together, and a bag of sealable snack bags. I cut the appropriate length of cord, sorted the beads into some inspirational words, and placed them into separate snack bags. I chose words like:

- Cherished
- Beautiful
- Treasured
- Talented
- Amazing
- Phenomenal
- Incredible
- Valued
- Wonderful
- Awesome
- Courageous
- Overcomer
- Faithful

When we met at a local restaurant, I let them choose a prepared snack bag and told them that it was their task to decipher the word to see just how God saw them. As we waited for our meal, they delighted in decoding their word, stringing it on the provided cord, and tying it on their wrists. (Yes, a couple of ladies dropped a bead or two and we had to crawl under our table to retrieve them, eliciting a lot of laughs and some strange looks from the other diners.)

It gave each of us opportunity to express to the others how much we valued our friendships and the reminder that we are loved by friends and by God.

Why don't you try that with your friends or family?

Building Together

It seems that much of what brings us together as friends involves food. I suppose it has been that way in this big world for centuries. Even Jesus seemed to find fellowship around a meal, so we find that to be a valid reason for the food that is usually on the table in front of us.

Meeting at a restaurant, I could tell the girls were waiting to see what "surprise" I had prepared for them. Never to disappoint, I presented several packages of inexpensive Lego-type blocks I had picked up at the Dollar Tree Store. (Yes, it is one of my favorite places to buy the necessary items for my creative ideas.)

We laughed about how many of those blocks we had stepped on in the middle of the night when we were raising our active little ones and the many places we had discovered them: in pants pockets, the washer or dryer, the dog's bed, deep inside the sofa, and, of course, the toilet!

But what would we do with them today?

We build.

We build homes.

And so, as we built a house (waiting for our meal, of course), we talked about how God had helped us to build homes for our families.

We shared some difficulties in the building of them: differences of opinion, strong-willed children, financial obstacles, and even the hardships of life that challenged our faith.

Our final thought before we consumed the last mozzarella stick was that the houses were well-constructed simply because we had let God be our General Contractor and we were just the obedient workers who had followed His orders.

Build a house with your friends or family. Let God open up the conversation and see where it leads.

But make sure there is some food on the table.

THANKFUL FOR YOU

I look forward to opportunities to meet with friends. We laugh a lot and catch up on what is happening in our individual worlds, giving encouragement and sharing concerns and successes. Smiles abound as does the love between us. We've been known to spew our coffee across the table as we have reacted to the unexpected joke or choke on our lunch at some hilarious situation. There are a lot of those "remember when…" moments, followed by peals of laughter.

I want you to know how much I cherish the friendship we share. As I step back and ponder why we enjoy this amazing communion, I believe it is because we are "positive speakers" in an often negative world.

I pray that this small lip balm will be a reminder of God's Word that reaffirms what we choose to live:

- "From the fruit of his lips a man is filled with good things as surely as the work of his hands rewards him." Proverbs 12:14
- "May the words of my mouth and the meditation of my heart be pleasing in your sight, O Lord, my Rock and my Redeemer." Psalm 19:14
- "The mouth of the righteous is a fountain of life." Proverbs 10:11a
- "The lips of the righteous nourish many…" Proverbs10:32a

- "Set a guard over my mouth, O Lord; keep watch over the door of my lips." Psalm 141:3
- "Kings take pleasure in honest lips; they value a man who speaks the truth." Proverbs 16:13
- "From the fruit of his mouth a man's stomach is filled; with the harvest from his lips he is satisfied." Proverbs 18:20

In this season of Thanksgiving, know that I am thankful for you, my treasured friend.

Suggestion: This can be accompanied by a small lip balm and can easily be adapted to Christmas, birthday, or a 'just because' greeting.

PRISMS

When you initially look at this prism, it is just an ordinary hunk of glass. There's really nothing special at all about it. Well, that is until light shines through it.

Do you remember the high school science class when the teacher produced a huge prism, turned down the room lights, and shot a ray of light onto the prism? We were amazed as we watched that incredible light show. You see, when light penetrates a prism, like a finely cut diamond, the light is internally reflected (bounces off the inside walls and angles) and then is transmitted through the front of the diamond. That's the "fire" of the diamond, especially a diamond that has been very finely cut, the rough edges removed, and a beautiful symmetry established. It absolutely amazes me that even though the light is the same and never changes, the reflection itself can change so much, revealing just what the light consists of.

The white light, when it is refracted in the prism, is deflected, broken down, and a beautiful spectrum of colors is produced. The order is always the same: red first, then orange, yellow, green, blue, and violet, all with their many hues and tones. For something that doesn't look as though it has much inside, it can surely set off a light show that will take your breath away.

Our lives are like this prism. Alone, we are just an ordinary hunk of glass, nothing special. But when we let the pure, white light of Jesus shine deep into us, when we allow Him (usually in times of crisis, illness, or broken relationships) to chip away at the rough edges of who we are and let Him create in us a beautiful symmetry, then, as He is refracted through our lives, the spectrum of colors of all that He is can be seen by others. Those colors can represent His attributes: love, peace, mercy, forgiveness, joy, patience, understanding, purity, power, wisdom, strength, holiness.

It's quite all right that we start off ordinary and lifeless. But we can't stay that way, because the Creator wants to mold us so that we can reflect an image of beauty, purity and holiness in this world. This prism reminds me of that and it tells me that I must hold myself to a higher standard, to allow Him to keep chipping away at all that would keep the world from clearly seeing Him live through me.

I want to let Him shine in me, to be the "fire" in me, to shine into the deepest part of who I am. I want Him to change me, mold me, and let me show the world who He is by how I live. It's amazing to see what the white Light of Jesus can do through something so very ordinary, like me. I need to be reminded of that.

Suggestion: Speaking to a group of ladies, I presented each one with a prism-like piece of glass. We later shared how God had brought us together with a purpose. How about making a purchase of a few prisms and invite some gal friends in to visit?

COMMONPLACE THINGS

Each year we come to this time when we recognize the opportunity before us to share, not only our most profound wishes for this Christmas season, but much more importantly, the very reason that we celebrate it. And each year we search for a fresh way, a unique and creative manner, that we can share in a way that will catch your attention, make you sit up, and clearly see that the whole of life begins and finds purpose here.

But the absolutely incredible truth is filled with such commonplace things:

- An ordinary town with common, ordinary people
- A humble carpenter and his young bride seeking to make a home where God is honored
- The birth of a baby
- A government ordered census
- Shepherds out doing what shepherds always do

Just common things.

And we are tempted to give little attention to the story for it is, at that point, so very much like our own lives….just ordinary.

But the extraordinary plan of God for His creation unfolds in the ordinary:

- The appearance of angels who spoke to men, lost and in need of a redeemer
- The birth of hope
- A star and the men who would abandon all to follow it in search of the long-awaited Promise
- A Savior who would be our "show and tell" on how to live, to love, and how to experience the eternal.

The truth of that Divine Plan has changed our lives. It has transformed us, brought us hope, given us strength, shown us an incomparable joy, given direction to our lives, opened our eyes to eternity and impassioned us to share it now with you.

We pray that you will, in the quiet of the day, pull out God's Word, open it to the Gospel of Luke and read again the story of Jesus. Let it invade your mind and carry you to the heart of the Father who is waiting to show you who He is and where He wants to lead you in the New Year.

That is our powerful desire for you, that you seek Him daily, love Him deeply, and serve Him faithfully until that day that He returns again.

Wishing you the presence of Christ in Christmas,

A Christmas Wish for You

All journeys require times of refreshment,
... time to sit back and reflect,
... time to plan for the road ahead,
... time to share what we have with others.
We must journey together.
Looking forward to the journey in the year to come as we journey with Jesus,

Immanuel.... "God is with us

The thought, that truth, grips us. It causes our hearts to race and our hopes to soar.
What more could we desire, in this season and each day of every year, than to have
God Himself with us? Immanuel...
It is true. He is with you. Let that vivid truth change your Christmas and the
course of the New Year. Imagine... God is with you!
Have a wonderful Christmas and a New Year overflowing with His blessings!
Trusting Him to do incredible things for you and through you,

Suggestion: These are perfect to insert in your Christmas greetings to your friends and family.

My Gift At Christmas

I wanted to give each of you, my friends, a gift for Christmas, but I wanted it to be something meaningful, something with lasting value, something that you could carry with you every day of the New Year and always. But I found that the things I wanted to give you were things I could not give you, for they are not tangible things.

I would like to give you **faith**. Not faith in man, but faith in God. To trust Him unequivocally when your world seems dark and you are confused or hurt or disillusioned. He will not leave you or forsake you. I have proven that over and over again in the dark times of my life.

I would like to give you **hope**. We all need it. Just listening to the evening news or reading the daily newspaper is sufficient to open our eyes to all the need that surrounds us. Emotional. Physical. Spiritual. God's word says that He sent us hope when He sent Jesus Christ into the world. I am so glad that I have that hope within me.

I would like to give you **peace**. Not just the peace that you feel on a restful day, but a deep, profound peace that passes all human comprehension. It is a peace that comes from God. It is a peace that doesn't waver when it seems that your world is crumbling, a peace that cannot be shaken by men's insults or economic crisis. It is that very peace that sustains me.

I would like to give you **assurance**. Assurance that all is well in your life. Not the assurance of man, for that is weak and faulty. But God's assurance for your future and for eternity. It is a wonderful thing to have this assurance. <u>No one</u> can take it away from me and only I can toss it aside if I decide to live my life my way instead of God's way.

I would like to give these things to you, <u>but I can't</u>. Nevertheless, I want you to know that <u>you can</u> have them all. God Himself is the giver of these valuable gifts and I hope you will ponder not just their availability but also the love of the One who offers them to you.

So, I would like to make this message my gift to you, as well as my friendship, a word of encouragement and hope, a listening ear, something to smile about when you are low, and my wishes to you for a Merry Christmas and a New Year filled with all the good things of God.

Seasons

Summer is over.
Another season passed
Almost imperceptibly.
I feel the coolness of new winds
And know that before I realize it
Autumn will be gone
And winter will enter like a storm.

There is a certain sadness as the seasons slip quickly and quietly by. There have been so many. And yet, I find profound joy in the memories of what would seem insignificant, easily forgettable moments:

- A child's shy birthday smile
- A kitchen filled with the aroma of a little girl's first culinary cookie success
- The infectious laughter of little children at play and the explosive roar of my husband as he watches a comedy
- The happy morning dance of a child who has discovered a gift from the tooth fairy
- The unique and unforgettable aroma of the wriggly, new puppy the neighbor introduced

- The sight of a teenager lost in a good book and the hungry look as he satisfyingly gorges his soul with the contents
- The birthday card from my elderly dad that read on the front, "The test results are in..", and on the inside, "You're old!" Dad is almost 94!

But we, my friends, have enjoyed many seasons together. We have shared our laughter and our tears. We have given and received wise counsel and trusted in the God who brought us together as friends.

You bless me and I, just because I am thanking God now for your friendship, wanted to share that with you.

I love and appreciate you.

Pillow Project Thanks

Sometimes a silly 'Thank You' is in order. After a pillow project for our local church, each lady that participated received this note:

Ain't nothin' like a 'piller'
With lots and lots of filler
To lay your weary noggin' on, you see.
But far better, I'm a knowin'
The love that's in your sewin',
And I thank you from the deepest part of me.

Oh, the filler it was flowin'
As the 'piller' pile was growin'
And you ladies sewed with love those works of art.
And I saw a bunch of grinnin'
As you went on with your pinnin',
Makin' 'pillers' with your hands and with your hearts.

Thank you for your help with the pillow project. The residents at our local nursing home will be warmed by them and by the love with which you made them. It was a lot of fun, wasn't it? Let's do it again soon.

My Prayer For You

Thank you for being a believer in the art of encouragement! You know the power of the simple gesture of extending that word that gives hope and confidence to others. You are among those who transform our world as you see opportunities in your sphere of influence and then take action to create positive change.

I pray that God will empower you and open your eyes wider to the value of fearlessly stepping into the lives of others and allowing God to speak through you. It is His gift of empowerment that compels you in compassion and concern to be the catalyst that carries someone from darkness to light, feeling lost to being found, confusion to assurance, and feeling unworthy to knowing there is value and purpose for every life.

Most of all, I pray that you will continue to deepen a meaningful relationship with the greatest encourager of all, Jesus Christ. Everything that we need, for this world and for the one to come, is found in only Him.

I Thessalonians 5:11 says it well: "Therefore, encourage one another and build each other up, just as in fact you are doing."

About Aleta

Aleta Harris and her husband of half a century have two adult children (plus five amazing grandchildren) and lives in Spring Hill, Florida. Her journey has taken her from a small coal mining community in Pennsylvania to a lifetime of ministry in the United States and South America as missionary, pastor's wife, teacher, writer, and nominal cook/housekeeper. Along the way, she has learned the indispensable blessing of encouraging others and being encouraged by them, something she trusts the reader will find warmly interlaced in the fruit of her pen.

Printed in the USA
CPSIA information can be obtained
at www.ICGtesting.com
LVHW011212040824
787161LV00002B/2

9 781400 325030